In memory of Drona

Balarama

A Royal Elephant

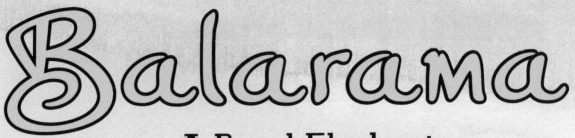

Caldecott Honor Winners

TED AND BETSY LEWIN

Lee & Low Books Inc. • *New York*

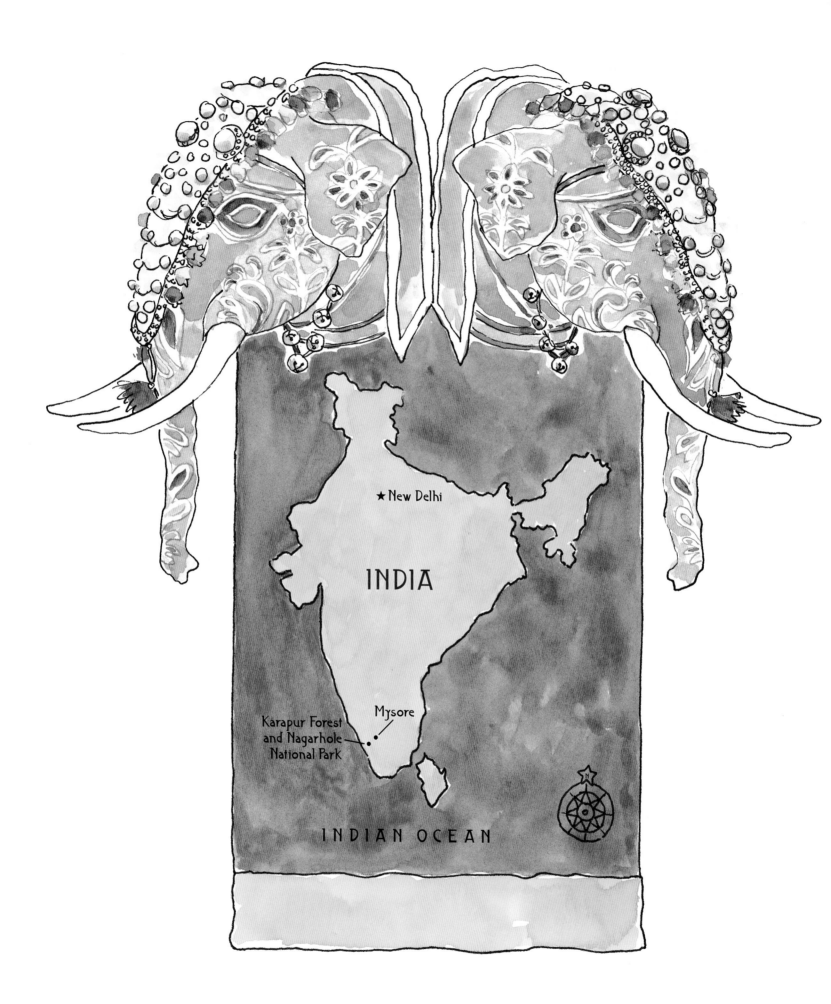

★ New Delhi

INDIA

Mysore

Karapur Forest
and Nagarhole
National Park

INDIAN OCEAN

Huge and magnificent, elephants stir the imagination like no other animal on Earth. In India these mammoth creatures are honored and admired, and for centuries they have been a part of religious, cultural, and social life throughout the country.

In years past the elephants of the Karapur Forest in southern India were in great demand. Maharajas, the Hindu kings of the land, wanted trained elephants for public festivities, and local people needed them for heavy work. From the 1880s until about 1970, roundups were used to capture elephants in pit traps called *kheddas*. A very large, deep pit was dug and covered with a thin layer of branches and leaves. When a herd of wild elephants was spotted, dozens of men using drums, gongs, fire, and firecrackers would drive the elephants into the pit. Once the elephants fell into the khedda, the area was surrounded by a stockade made of stout logs lashed together. After a week or two in the khedda, the elephants were pulled out with the help of logs and already-tamed elephants ridden by their *mahouts*, or trainers. Only then did the process of training the exhausted, dazed creatures begin.

Because of the pain and suffering inflicted on the elephants, kheddas are outlawed now. Today great herds of these giant wild animals move peacefully through the Karapur Forest. The forest is also home to many camp, or trained, elephants that are used for festivals and work. Some of these elephants were captured before the kheddas became illegal. Others have been born to camp elephants. The animals are cared for and trained by their mahouts, who live side by side with the elephants in the forest. Mahouts have a deep, lifelong connection with their animals. The sons of mahouts often become elephant trainers too.

The greatest of all the camp elephants are the Royal Elephants.

ELEPHANT CAMP

From the city of Mysore we head out with a car and driver for the Karapur Forest near Nagarhole National Park. We are on our way to see the elephants of southern India. We drive under an arch of banyan trees planted years ago by the maharaja as a place for weary travelers to rest out of the blazing sun. Palm tree-lined rice paddies border the road for miles.

In the Karapur Forest we meet up with our guide, Sundar, and take off in his open jeep. Before long a lumbering elephant and her calf appear on the track ahead. The bell hanging loosely from her neck makes a haunting, mournful sound. The elephant has a fresh wound on her belly. She was out in the forest the night before foraging for food and was attacked by an aggressive bull elephant. It's a deep puncture wound from the bull's tusk, but the elephant's mahout says she will be all right.

The elephant stops next to our jeep. From our seats we look into one of her huge brown eyes.

"We've never looked into an elephant's eye before," we say. The long, thick broom of her lashes descends and rises in a slow, solemn blink.

We follow the two elephants as they plod on to the camp, a group of mud huts with tiled roofs deep in the forest. There are five more elephants in the camp being cared for by their mahouts.

At one end of the camp is a small temple with elephant
bells hanging from the eaves. Painted on the doorstep of the
temple is a *rangoli*, a symbol of good luck and welcome.
Women in bright, colorful clothes carry jugs of water
on their heads. They walk slowly past the elephants
and into their houses.

There is a young elephant in the camp that already weighs about eight hundred pounds. "He's a little handful of mischief," Sundar says.

The elephant loves to chase the children, bowling them over and making them scatter as he runs through the camp.

Sundar stands in the smoke drifting up from a big pot of elephant mash that smells like baking bread. The mash is a mixture of water, salt, millet, and graham flour. It is very nutritious, and the children love it as much as the elephants.

The mahouts' children surround Sundar. They know by heart the story he is about to tell. We join them.

"Drona, the lead Royal Elephant, is very clever. He loves bananas. He knows that every week a big truck loaded with bananas comes up the forest road. One day, as soon as Drona smelled the bananas, he walked to the road and waited near the top of a hill. Drona watched as the truck came slowly into view. Nearing the top of the hill, the driver shifted gears and pushed down on the gas pedal. Nothing happened. The truck wouldn't budge. The driver and his helper couldn't understand why they weren't moving forward. Then the driver glanced into the rearview mirror, and all he saw was elephant! Drona had grabbed the back of the truck with his trunk and was holding the truck in place. The men were so frightened, they leaped from the cab and ran into the forest. Drona then tipped over the truck and ate all but one case of the bananas."

The children laugh as if they were hearing the story for the first time. We ask Sundar if we could see Drona. He says Drona is at another camp near the Kabini River. He will take us there.

During our drive to the camp, Sundar tells us that Drona
is a mighty tusker. He was chosen many years ago as the
Ambari elephant, the highest honor an elephant can receive.
The Ambari elephant is the lead Royal Elephant of the
maharaja of Mysore's annual parade through the city on
the last day of Dasara, a centuries-old royal and religious
festival. The last day commemorates the Hindu goddess
Chamundeshwari and celebrates the triumph of good over evil.
Drona was selected as the Ambari elephant mostly for his
distinctive aura, the special energy that radiates from him. At
the camp we are met by Drona's mahout. He tells us to wait,
then disappears into the forest. He returns talking softly
to the huge beast at his side. Drona's forehead is massive,
his tusks thick and pointed. He faces us and his ears come
forward. He is magnificent. We feel his aura strongly.

"Drona is very friendly to everyone," Sundar says. "But
you should see him when he carries 'the gold.' He takes on
a royal attitude then. He even walks with a different gait.
It's as if he is telling the other elephants to follow him."

We decide that we must return the following year to
see Drona carry the gold.

ONE YEAR LATER

We are back in southern India for Dasara and are looking forward to seeing Drona lead the parade. But when we meet up with Sundar, he has bad news.

"I'm sorry to tell you that Drona is dead," Sundar says. "He was feeding along the road near the elephant camp. There was plenty to eat everywhere. Why he decided to graze near the road instead of in the forest, who knows?"

Drona had pulled down a large tree branch in order to eat the leaves. The falling branch struck an electrical line, and Drona was electrocuted. Everyone in Mysore was saddened. His mahout and the others who lived in the elephant camp were devastated. They felt as if they had lost their best friend.

"Would you like to see Drona's grave?" Sundar asks.

"Yes, very much," we say.

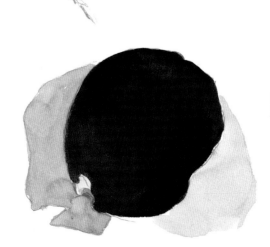

Sundar drives us to a high, lush bank overlooking the Kabini River.
There, Drona's grave is marked with a large, three tiered pink marble tablet.
Drona's huge body was buried beneath the stone. Offerings of wildflowers
are scattered atop the grave.

We feel as if we too have lost a friend. We stand quietly for a while, then
place our own wildflowers among the others.

The next day in Mysore we meet Nagaraj, our official guide for Dasara. He offers to introduce us to Balarama, the elephant chosen to take Drona's place. It will be Balarama's first time leading the maharaja's parade, his first time carrying the golden *howdah*—an eight-hundred-pound ceremonial carriage made of wood sheathed in gold. Inside sits a statue of the goddess Chamundeshwari.

It's a short walk from our hotel to the maharaja's palace, where the parade will begin.

"Some people think there will never be another Ambari elephant like Drona," says Nagaraj. "Balarama may not have the aura of Drona, but he's an impressive animal."

We follow along as Nagaraj leads us across the palace grounds to the stables. Balarama was brought here from the forest a few days ago to get used to the city. At first Balarama's mahout does not want to let us see the prized elephant in his charge. He steps in front of the stall's small, barred window and waves us away.

Nagaraj holds out his official badge and the mahout relents. He opens the large stable door and calls quietly to the elephant within. Slowly Balarama emerges. He peeks out, high above us. Then his brightly painted head and shoulders appear. He is *very* impressive. We back away in awe.

Balarama breathes heavily. He sways back and forth. His presence is overwhelming. Hearts pounding, we back away still farther and nod "okay" to the mahout. He seems relieved as Balarama slowly retreats into his stall.

We think Balarama has *plenty* of aura.

DRESSING OF THE ELEPHANTS

Leaving Balarama behind, we step outside.

A high wall with four towering entry gates surrounds seventy-eight acres of beautifully landscaped grounds. In the center sits a magnificent palace that is home to the maharaja of Mysore and his family.

Along one wall by a grove of trees, the mahouts have pitched their tents. They are cooking over open fires, preparing large balls of elephant mash. The brightly painted elephants are chained to trees to keep them from wandering off. Children run over and stuff the mash into the waiting mouths of the elephants.

A short while later, the mahouts mount their elephants, then amble over to a shady courtyard in a corner of the palace grounds. Gorgeous silk and satin drapes dazzle us as they are thrown over the elephants and spill down their sides.

Once the elephants are dressed they are led off to a marble pool shaded by huge mango trees. The animals drink their fill of the cool, refreshing water.

BALARAMA, THE AMBARI ELEPHANT

"Look! Look! Balarama is coming!" the crowd shouts.

The majestic Balarama and his mahout slowly cross the palace grounds and enter the dressing area. Standing on a platform at the base of a tree, Balarama's mahout gently embraces the elephant's huge head, the tusks extending like ivory railings on either side. The mahout strokes Balarama's eyelashes, while the tip of the elephant's trunk whisks nervously back and forth on the ground.

The dressing begins. Silken drapes are spread over Balarama, then the golden howdah is placed on his back. Mahouts position Balarama below special equipment that gently lowers the howdah. It is a slow, delicate task.

Balarama's big moment is fast approaching. We are excited and nervous for him. It is important that he stay calm and not be distracted by the crowds and noise. We hope Balarama will make a good impression in his debut as the Ambari elephant.

Finally, under a blazing sun, the ceremony begins. *Clip, clop. Clip, clop.* First come the mounted police guards—turbaned riders carrying long, flag-topped lances, sitting tall and straight in their saddles. Then units of cadets, soldiers, and more police guards pour into the big square in front of the palace.

All units snap to attention. Excitement hangs in the superheated air. Onlookers crane their necks to see.

Then there he is—*Balarama*—carrying the golden howdah!

Balarama's mahout turns him to face the stage full of dignitaries in front of the palace. After the chief minister performs a *puja*, a ritual blessing, the crowd cheers, tossing flowers in the air and all over Balarama.

When the ceremony ends, Balarama turns and faces the people packed into the palace grounds. The howdah sways and sparkles in the sunlight. Balarama's big moment is about to begin.

Balarama moves majestically toward one of the palace gates, leading a mile-long procession. Band after band and unit after unit of guards and soldiers march smartly past the stage, following Balarama onto the packed streets of Mysore. Throngs of people push forward to see Balarama in his first ceremonial parade.

We are bursting with pride. He is doing great.

THUMP
THUMP

Next come the performers.

Colorfully costumed stilt walkers strut by as dancers wildly twirl and leap to the beat of a dozen drums.

BOOM
BOOM
BOOM

BOOM BA-BOOM

Men stage fierce fights with long bamboo sticks to the sharp
sounds of wood on wood.

CLACK
CLACK

CRACK
CRACK

A final line of elephants appears, their silk drapes shimmering in the brilliant light. The last of the parade files through the palace gate. Caught up in the thrill and excitement of the spectacle, we join the crush of people moving out into the street.

THE DAY AFTER

It is early morning on the palace grounds. Balarama, his big day over, is quietly feeding outside the stables. The splendid paintings on his body have faded. His mahout squats at his feet.

We walk up close.

"You did a good job, Balarama," we say. At the sound of our voices Balarama turns toward us. His ears flap softly and his trunk whisks slowly back and forth. With each breath, little puffs of dust rise from the ground. He looks so peaceful and contented.

Later we see an article in *The Times of India*. Balarama is front-page news. The caption under his picture in the newspaper reads "Elephant Balarama, chosen to carry the golden 'howdah' for the first time in the Mysore Dasara procession, gave a flawless performance."

We cut out Balarama's photograph from the paper to remind us of this glorious event. We also think about Drona, and how for a whole year we had looked forward to seeing him carry "the gold." But now Balarama has won the hearts of all who saw him proudly carrying the golden howdah. He is truly the Ambari elephant, the greatest of the Royal Elephants.

ELEPHANT FACTS

Elephants are the largest animals that live on land. They are found in both Asia and Africa. All elephants are endangered. Centuries of hunting and habitat destruction have caused severe declines in their numbers. In India today, protecting elephant populations is important for their survival, and to the country's rich cultural, social, and religious heritage.

Asian elephants, also known as Indian elephants, and African elephants vary in several physical characteristics.

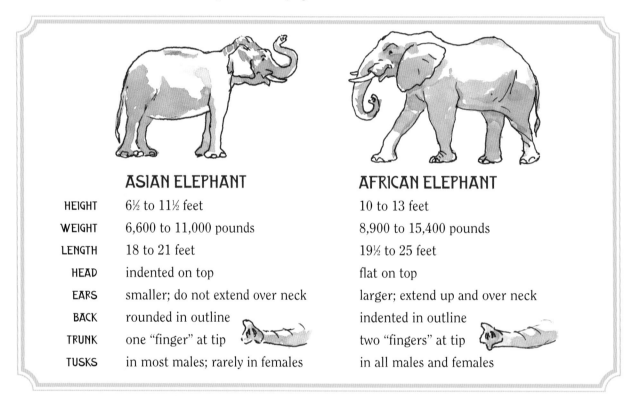

	ASIAN ELEPHANT	AFRICAN ELEPHANT
HEIGHT	6½ to 11½ feet	10 to 13 feet
WEIGHT	6,600 to 11,000 pounds	8,900 to 15,400 pounds
LENGTH	18 to 21 feet	19½ to 25 feet
HEAD	indented on top	flat on top
EARS	smaller; do not extend over neck	larger; extend up and over neck
BACK	rounded in outline	indented in outline
TRUNK	one "finger" at tip	two "fingers" at tip
TUSKS	in most males; rarely in females	in all males and females

An elephant's trunk has tens of thousands of individual muscles. Elephants use their trunks to tear down large tree limbs *and* to pick up tiny objects. They also use their trunks to squirt water over their backs and into their mouths, and to blow dirt over their backs during dust baths.

Elephants fan their ears to cool off. The fanning creates a breeze that cools the blood vessels near the surface of the ears. The cooled blood then circulates to the rest of the body. In the hottest part of the day, elephants often seek out the water or the shade of trees.

Tusks are elongated, greatly enlarged teeth. Just as humans are right-handed or left-handed, elephants are right-tusked or left-tusked. Elephants use their tusks to dig for water, salt, and roots, and to move trees and branches out of their way. Tusks are also used as weapons when fighting.

Elephants have wide, padded feet, so in spite of their great size and weight, they are able to walk quietly. They walk at a speed of about 4 miles per hour and can run for short distances.

Elephants are vegetarians, and they travel long distances in search of food. Adults eat about 300 pounds of food a day. In the wild, their diet includes grasses, herbs, leaves, roots, bark, and fruits. Elephants also drink between 19 and 24 gallons of water daily.

Elephants communicate via growls, rumbles, bellows, and moans. Some of these low-frequency sounds may travel more than a mile. Elephants also trumpet loudly when they are excited, surprised, anxious, or attacking.

Female elephants give birth every three to six years, depending on the habitat. They are pregnant for twenty to twenty-two months. Usually only one calf is born.

Elephant calves weigh between 200 and 300 pounds at birth and are about 3 feet tall. They are able to stand and walk two hours after they are born.

Female and young male elephants live in herds of related adults and their offspring. The oldest female is usually in charge. Males leave the herd when they are around thirteen years old and travel alone or in groups with other young males.

Elephants live to be between fifty and seventy years old.

Royal Elephants of the Mysore Dasara

The participation of elephants is a central part of the Mysore Dasara celebration. The stories of the Royal Elephants, especially the Ambari elephants, are part of local history and legends. These are the most recent lead elephants.

Biligiriranga was a majestic animal, about 10 feet tall with tusks 2 feet long. He was a grand-looking animal and was reported to have increased the glory of the Mysore Dasara during the mid-twentieth century. Biligiriranga was loyal and always obedient to his mahout.

Rajendra was caught in 1971. Although he served as the lead elephant, he was said to have been easily influenced and distracted from his duties by the presence of female elephants. His mahouts felt that Rajendra was always looking for a compatible mate and never found "true love."

Drona was introduced to the Dasara festivities in 1982. He was a massive animal with a unique, innate ability to move his muscles selectively to adjust for the shifting weight of the golden howdah during the procession. Drona attained almost celebrity status because of his graceful gait and gentle behavior. One day in 1998 Drona went grazing and pulled down a branch so he could eat the leaves. The falling branch also brought down a power line, and Drona was electrocuted instantly.

Arjuna was the elephant being trained to succeed Drona. Arjuna and another elephant went to bathe in a river one day. While crossing a road, the elephants were startled by a noisy vehicle. In the chaos that followed, the other elephant's mahout fell and was accidentally trampled and killed by Arjuna. People felt that an elephant that had killed a person was not fit to participate in the Dasara festivities.

Balarama began carrying the golden howdah in 1998. At first some people felt he was not outgoing enough. He also needed special training so he could withstand the noise of the loud canon fire that occurs during the parade. Balarama overcame these problems and became a star attraction of the Mysore Dasara. He led the procession for the eleventh time in October 2008. At fifty years old, the elephant's strength and physical abilities were not quite what they used to be. A new lead elephant may soon take Balarama's place.

GLOSSARY and PRONUNCIATION GUIDE

This guide provides pronunciations for English words as well as approximations for the pronunciations of Hindi and Kannada words. Hindi is a language spoken widely in India, and Kannada is the language spoken in the Mysore region of the country. All syllables in Hindi and Kannada are stressed equally.

Ambari (am-bahr-ee): lead Royal Elephant in the Mysore Dasara

Arjuna (ahr-ju-nah): name of an Ambari elephant

aura (OR-uh): energy field that surrounds a living being

Balarama (bahl-ah-rah-mah): name of an Ambari elephant

banyan (BAN-yen): tree with branches that have hanging roots which grow down to the soil and start new trunks

Biligiriranga (bil-ee-ghee-ree-rahn-gah): name of an Ambari elephant

bull (bul): adult male animal

cadet (keh-DET): young person in training to be a military officer

calf (kaf): young of various large animals

Chamundeshwari (chaa-moon-day-shwuh-ree): Hindu goddess representing the triumph of good over evil

Dasara (dah-sayr-ah *or* dah-sah-rah): centuries-old, ten-day Hindu festival celebrated in India

debut (DEY-byoo *or* dey-BYOO): first appearance

Drona (droh-nah): name of an Ambari elephant

eave (eeve): lower edge of a roof that overhangs the wall

electrocute (eh-LEK-truh-kyut): to kill by electric shock

forage (FOR-ij): to hunt or search for food

gait (gayt): manner of walking or moving

graham flour (GRAY-uhm FLOU-er): whole wheat flour

Hindu (HIN-doo): person who believes in Hinduism; person born or living in India

Hinduism (HIN-doo-IZ-uhm): religion, philosophy, and social system native to and common in India

howdah (hau-dah): seat or carriage carried on an elephant's back

Kabini River (kah-been-ee): river that runs through the Karapur Forest

Karapur Forest (kar-ah-por): forest in the southern part of India near Nagarhole National Park

khedda (khed-uh): pit trap used in southern India to capture wild elephants

lance (lahns): long spear with a pointed metal tip

maharaja (mah-huh-rah-juh): Hindu king

mahout (meh-hoot): person who cares for and trains an elephant

mammoth (MAM-uhth): of very great size, huge

mash (mash): mixture of grains and water

Mysore (my-sawr): city in southern India

Nagaraj (nah-gah-raj): man's name

Nagarhole National Park (nah-gahr-hoh-lay): park in southern India, near Mysore

procession (pruh-SESH-uhn): group moving along in an orderly way

puja (pooh-jah): in Hinduism, a ceremonial worship or blessing

Rajendra (rah-jen-druh): name of an Ambari elephant

rangoli (rahn-goh-lee): floor painting created from colored powders; traditional sign of welcome

Royal Elephant (ROI-uhl EL-uh-fent): elephant that participates in the Dasara procession

stockade (stah-KADE): enclosure or pen made with posts and stakes

Sundar (sun-dahr): man's name

tusk (tuhsk): elongated tooth that extends from the mouth of an animal

tusker (TUHS-ker): animal that has tusks

Authors' Sources

This story is based on actual events that took place in and around Mysore, India, in January 1997 and September and October 1998. Much of the research was conducted while the authors were in India and encompasses their primary experiences and observations, including conversations with guides and local experts there.

"Animals: Elephant Museum." Oregon Zoo,
　　http://www.oregonzoo.org/Cards/Elephants/elephant.museum.htm

"Animals: Mammals." National Geographic,
　　http://animals.nationalgeographic.com/animals/mammals

Kumar, R. Krishna. "Balarama to carry the golden howdah." *The Hindu*. October 20,
　　2007, http://www.hindu.com/2007/10/20/stories/2007102054760500.htm

Mallikarjuna, D.G., and Vikas Kanat, trans. "The Elephants of Mysore Dasara." Kamat's
　　Potpourri, http://www.kamat.com/kalranga/prani/elephants/dasara_elephants.htm

Mysore Dasara, http://mysoredasara.com/Dasara/

Smithsonian National Zoological Park. Search "Asian elephant," http://nationalzoo.si.edu

WWF (World Wildlife Fund). Search "Asian elephant" and "African elephant,"
　　http://www.panda.org

Acknowledgments

Many thanks to Sundar, wildlife manager, Kabini River Lodge, Karnataka, India. Thanks also to Darrin Lunde, Collections Manager, Department of Mammalogy, American Museum of Natural History; Uma Krishnaswami, children's book author and codirector of Bisit Writing Project, a site of the National Writing Project; and Rani Iyer, freelance writer, for reviewing the manuscript and for their valuable input.

　　Photograph on p. 49 of Balarama leading the Mysore Dasara procession from *The Times of India*, Bangalore edition, October 2, 1998. Used with permission.

Manufactured in China

Book design by Susan and David Neuhaus/NeuStudio
Book production by The Kids at Our House

The text is set in Clearface
The full-color illustrations are rendered in watercolor on Strathmore bristol board. The spot illustrations are rendered in reed pen and sumi ink with watercolor washes, also on Strathmore bristol board.

10 9 8 7 6 5 4 3 2 1
First Edition

Library of Congress Cataloging-in-Publication Data
Lewin, Ted.
Balarama : a royal elephant / Ted and Betsy Lewin. — 1st ed.
　　p. cm.
　　Summary: "World travelers Ted and Betsy Lewin recount how the trained elephants of southern India, in particular the one chosen to be the lead elephant in the Mysore Dasara, are raised, cared for, and prepared for performing in ceremonial processions. Includes background information and glossary"—Provided by publisher.
　　ISBN 978-1-60060-265-8 (hardcover : alk. paper)
1. Asiatic elephant—India—Mysore—Juvenile literature. 2. Asiatic elephant—Training—India—Nagarhole National Park—Juvenile literature. I. Lewin, Betsy. II. Title.
QL737.P98L49 2009
636.9670954'87—dc22　　　　　　　　　　　　　　　　　　　　　　　　　　2009001499